It's Only Pretend

Oliver really wants to play a princess in Ariana's story. He stops, confused, when some of the other boys laugh. But when Noah, the new boy, refuses to take any notice of the laughter, Oliver discovers that there is another way...

This beautifully illustrated story book explores a common situation that arises for children and teachers taking part in Helicopter Stories and allows the children to explore their feelings in a sensitive and supportive environment. The story is accompanied by teacher's notes on how to use the book with young children along with questions and discussion prompts that can be incorporated into the curriculum.

In a class where Helicopter Stories take place on a regular basis, It's Only Pretend explores issues around gender that might come up in story acting. It is part of the Helicopter Stories Tale series, a valuable and visually captivating resource for all Early Years educators using storytelling and story acting with their children.

Trisha Lee is a writer, theatre director and storyteller. She was the first to pioneer Helicopter Stories in the UK and she founded the theatre and education company MakeBelieve Arts in 2002.

Amie Taylor is a writer and artist. She founded her shadow puppetry and illustration company 'The Shadow Makers' in 2013 and now delivers workshops and projects in creating shadow work and illustration.

"These picture books bring to life the magic of Storytelling and Story Acting. The authentic examples and quandaries are compelling. Trisha gives advice based on her vast experience but also includes the voice of Vivian Gussin Paley herself. This book will be an invaluable resource for anyone who is developing the art of Helicopter Stories in their setting."

Anna Ephgrave, author of five books around the topic of "Planning in the Moment"

"Childhood deserves to spend its days in an immersive world of story and make-believe, and yet again, Trisha shows us how. The rich possibilities she has created here enable an exploration, not only of Helicopter Stories, but of who we are in the kingdom of play. A true adventure awaits you within its pages.

Holding hands with Trisha's words are the wonderful illustrations of Amie Taylor, that turn up the dial of imagination and invite us in to story dream even more."

Greg Bottrill, author of Can I Go and Play Now – Rethinking the Early Years *and* School and the Magic of Children

"Trisha Lee has written a lovely, accessible set of stories that can be dramatized through the Vivian Gussin Paley method. It is set in the classroom of Fiona Fable, who knows that every child has a story inside them, and her job is to find a way to let those stories out.

These stories bring to light the importance of children being able to tell their stories right here and right now. It's a beautiful and natural way of allowing children to address their worries, share their ideas and catch a glimpse of their imaginations.

We have used this approach for many years at LEYF [London Early Years Foundation], and it has made us so much more alert to the power of storytelling. Everyone has a story, and this book gives you the tools to make this part of your daily life of any classroom. It tells the teacher to watch very carefully, and you will see the children's stories dancing through the air. It is joyful."

June O'Sullivan, CEO of London Early Years Foundation, and author of numerous publications about the Early Years

It's Only Pretend
A Helicopter Stories Tale

TRISHA LEE ILLUSTRATED BY AMIE TAYLOR

Routledge
Taylor & Francis Group

LONDON AND NEW YORK

Cover image: Amie Taylor

First edition published 2023
by Routledge
4 Park Square, Milton Park, Abingdon, Oxon, OX14 4RN

and by Routledge
605 Third Avenue, New York, NY 10158

Routledge is an imprint of the Taylor & Francis Group, an informa business

British Library Cataloguing-in-Publication Data
A catalogue record for this book is available from the British Library

ISBN: 978-1-032-05383-7 (pbk)
ISBN: 978-1-003-19732-4 (ebk)

DOI: 10.4324/9781003197324

Typeset in Antitled
by Apex CoVantage, LLC

For Vivian

IT'S ONLY PRETEND

A HELICOPTER STORIES TALE

TRISHA LEE

ILLUSTRATED BY AMIE TAYLOR

David Fulton Book

Introduction

Helicopter Stories is based on the work of American kindergarten teacher and author Vivian Gussin Paley. It was pioneered in the UK by Trisha Lee and theatre and education company MakeBelieve Arts.

Helicopter Stories is, in theory, a simple approach; children tell their stories to an adult scribe, who writes their words verbatim on an A5 sheet of paper. These stories are then acted out around a taped out stage.

It's Only Pretend is based on a real life situation in an Early Years classroom. It presents a problem that I have seen many times alongside a solution that the children in one classroom found to overcome it. At the end of this book, you will find more information on the strategies I use to explore issues around gender with young children, alongside a copy of Ariana's story.

It's Only Pretend is suitable for children aged 3 to 7.

Fiona Fable's classroom **overflowed with stories**. She read them, told them and made them up. Best of all, the children got to make up their own stories too. Then they got to act them out.

"Once there were two princesses," said Ariana. She would be the first princess, and the rest of the class would take it in turn to play the other characters.

But when Oliver stood up to be the second princess, Patrik and Lucas laughed.

"I don't want to be a princess," said Oliver, sitting back down.

"It's only pretend," said Ariana. "You don't have to be a real princess. Just a made-up one."

"I want to be a dinosaur," said Oliver.
But there weren't any dinosaurs in Ariana's story.

Fiona Fable asked the other children in turn.
"Would you like to be the princess?"
"Would you like to be the princess?"
"Would you like to be the princess?"

"No thank you," said Jaden.

"No way," said Patrik.

"No!" said Lucas.

'When we act in each other's stories, we can be any character we like. It's only pretend,' said Fiona Fable.
'I'll do it,' said Daisy. 'I don't mind what character I am.

A monster. Raaah!

A baddy. Growl.

A spider. Tickle-tickle.
It's only pretend."

Oliver watched, wishing he
could be any character he liked.

"*The two princesses tiptoed through the **haunted forest**,*" read Ms Fable.

"*They splashed through the* **poisonous lake**."

"They climbed the **hazardous mount**

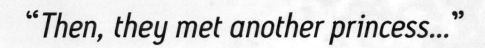
"Then, they met another princess..."

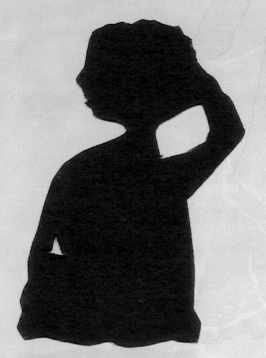

"Noah, do you want to be the other princess?" asked Ms Fable.

And Noah stood up.

Everyone gasped. Noah was new.
He didn't know the rules.

"Noah! No!" whispered Oliver.
"Boys can't be princesses!"

"The princesses danced," read Ms Fable.

Princess Ariana, Daisy and Noah **danced** and **giggled** and **giggled** and **danced**.

Oliver tapped his foot

"*Then, a big, red dragon came!*"
It was Ella's turn to join in.
"*The dragon breathed fire. It was trying to eat the princesses.*"

Ella spread her arms.
She flew around the three princesses,
roaring fiercely.

"*The princesses fought the dragon,*" read Ms Fable.
"Take that!" said Daisy, lashing at the air.

"And one of the princesses killed the dragon."
Daisy stabbed with her pretend sword, and Ella,
the dragon, fell to the floor.

"Everyone cheered."

The princesses **cheered**.

The audience **cheered**.

Lucas, Patrik and Oliver **cheered**.

The next day, it was Oliver's turn to tell a story.
"Once, there was a princess who hunted for dragons..."

"I'm going to be the princess," said Oliver.
"After all, it's only pretend..."

Teachers Notes - It's Only Pretend

"Relieved of the responsibility of looking for loopholes in the law, the children have an opposite reaction. If they cannot change the role, then they will accept any role. They dare to take on implausible roles, shyly at first, but after a while with great aplomb, as if accepting the challenge to eliminate their own stereotyped behaviours."

Vivian Gussin Paley — *You Can't Say You Can't Play*

Once you have read *It's Only Pretend* to your children, think about initiating a conversation with them, using some of the starting points below.

- I wonder what Oliver was thinking when he stood up to be a princess, and Patrik and Lucas laughed. What do you think?
- Tell me why Noah didn't sit down when the other children whispered to him that boys couldn't be princesses.
- What sort of things do princesses get up to in the story? What else might they do?
- What do you think happened in the story Oliver made up at the end of the book, where he decided he would be a princess?

Ask your children if they would like to act out Ariana's story.

Ariana's Story

Once there were two princesses. They tiptoed through the haunted forest. They splashed through the poisonous lake, and they climbed the hazardous mountain. Then they met another princess. The princesses danced. Then a big red dragon came. The dragon breathed fire. It was trying to eat the princesses. The princesses fought the dragon. One of the princesses killed the dragon. Everyone cheered.

When you act out this story, take it in turns to cast each character by going around the stage, just like they do in Fiona Fable's classroom. This way, gender roles will be blurred, and the characters will be cast based on where they are sitting. You could act the story out several times or have more than three princesses.

Here are some quick pointers to help with the acting out:

- Gather the children in a circle around a rectangular, taped out stage. Alternatively, get children to sit around the edges of your classroom carpet.
- Read the story, one line at a time, inviting individual children to become each of the characters and act out that segment of the story, before moving to the next sentence.
- At the end of the story, clap thank you, and everyone sits back down.

For more information on how to deliver Helicopter Stories, read Princesses, Dragons and Helicopter Stories by Trisha Lee, which is a how-to on the approach or visit https://helicopterstories.co.uk/courses/helicopter-stories-on-demand/

Once you have finished acting out the story, perhaps you could invite the children to act out some of the other things they think the princesses might do.

How do the princesses relax, after they have fought a dragon?

What do they have for dinner?

Where will they go for their next adventure?

When we act out a Helicopter Story, the child who made up the story is allowed to cast themselves in whichever role they would like. However, they are NOT permitted to cast any of the other children. The rest of the casting is done by going around the stage, child by child, side by side, inviting the next person in line to take the part. As a result, the role each child is offered is based on the random aspect of where they are sitting when that character is first mentioned. When inviting children to take part from their place around the stage, it is essential to remember one of the few rules of Helicopter Stories.

No child should be forced, coerced, or bribed to tell a story or to act out in a story.
Every child has the right to say no.

One of the strengths of taking it in turns around the stage is that gender roles become blurred. Girls become superheroes. Boys become princesses, and all of the children get the opportunity to be trees and castles and creaky doors. The role the child plays becomes less important; after all, it is only pretend.

Well, that is until someone says NO! or "Boys can't be princesses."

As demonstrated in *It's Only Pretend*, when this happens, we are suddenly greeted by a group of children shaking their heads and refusing to take on any role that they perceive as overtly female. Suddenly, our democratic circle crunches to a halt.

Of course, this doesn't happen to every group. I have worked with children in Preschool, Reception and Year 1, who happily get up to be Mummy or Batman or Peppa Pig or Mr Potato Head regardless of their gender. But it only takes one child to challenge this blurring of roles and that view can quickly circulate. Perhaps it starts with a shaking of the head, or it might be a mere murmur that this is not an appropriate role for them, and suddenly there is a refusal to join in from a group of that child's friends.

So, first, let us look deeper at this issue, and then I will suggest some strategies.

One of the things that I have noticed, having worked with thousands of children in hundreds of classrooms across the world, is that when the gender issue comes up, it is almost always brought up by a boy. The idea that it is not okay to be the princess, or Anna from Frozen, or a character with one of the same names as a girl in the class is something that boys seem to vocalise first.

Often, this objection to playing a perceived 'female role' starts with one of the boys stating in a loud voice that 'Boys can't be Princesses'. Other times it might start with a giggle between two or three of the boys. When this happens, the boy that stood up to take on the role of the princess often sits down, just like Oliver in our stories did, knowing that the laughter was directed at him.

It seems that it is harder for boys to take on roles that are more frequently linked to a different gender than it is for girls. Even at age four and five, boys who have had been subjected to very proscribed gender roles will already be beginning to feel that taking on a role meant for another gender is not an option for them.

By the age of 6 or 7, children will have been exposed to even more examples of fixed gender roles. If they haven't been doing Helicopter Stories before that age or been around adults who allow them to question these rigid frameworks, it is highly likely that this issue of not wanting to take on certain roles will arise.

Sally Veale, Vice Principal for Ashgrove Academy, Cheshire, a Helicopter Stories Champion, wrote about this issue in a blog she created for MakeBelieve Arts Helicopter Stories website in November 2019.

> *"The first time I really became aware of this issue was when the Disney film, Frozen was still a big deal. Many of the private stories told by the girls involved Anna and Elsa. Each girl in our acting circle would happily stand up, lift the sides of her imaginary skirt, and, along with her magical sister, begin the fantasy of building their snowman or forging a palace out of ice. Some of the boys, whilst more than happy to be the snowman, the ice giant or even the reindeer, were less than keen on being the princesses."*

The issue is as old as the hills. Boys play boy characters, girls play girl characters, but it doesn't have to be this way.

Having tracked groups of children doing Helicopter Stories from age 2 to 7, I have always found that as they get older, children in these groups are so used to playing whichever role is required that they take on any character, without giving it a second thought.

But what about the girls?

A few years ago, I probably would have said that this issue never presents itself for the girls. I have seen girls willingly get up to become bad guys, zombies, batman and spiderman, without a second thought about whether this is appropriate.

Once, there was a girl who I invited up to play Vilgax from Ben 10, who needed to ask me some questions before she acted out the role.

"What's my job? What do I do?" asked Jane, once the role had been assigned to her.

Michael, who had written the story, wasn't much help. "Vilgax is very tall, bigger than Ben 10, and he's grey," he replied.

Jane shook her head, "Yes, but what is my job? How do I know how to move if I don't know what I am supposed to be doing."

It was a great question, but Michael looked equally perplexed. So, I asked him if Vilgax was a goodie or a baddie.

"A baddie," replied Michael. Finally, Jane had enough information. She took to the stage and pulled a suitably mean face while she stamped around. She had found her motivation.

Can you imagine a boy asking for such precise information to enable him to play Elsa from Frozen or Maleficent from Sleeping Beauty? "What do I do? How do I hold my skirt?"

However, what I have seen from girls, on the rare occasion they refuse a role based on gender, is a self-conscious shaking of the head when asked to be a baddie or a robber or a superhero. The difference in this scenario is that often when a girl refuses to become a character that would usually be seen as male, it tends to be an individual choice, and it is not vocalised so loudly. This makes it easier to miss, and it also means that it doesn't impact the choices of the other children. But, on rare occasions, it is still there, and for both boys and girls, some roles that come up in stories might not be ones they want to play. All of which is fine. No child should ever be forced to act when they don't want to, but we need to find ways to open up the stage, and make all roles accessible to our children in a way that feels safe for them and where their choices are respected.

It's Just Pretend

One of the things that I often say to a group of children is that it is just pretend. When children act out on the stage, or when they make up stories through fantasy play, they are only pretending to be a character; they are not becoming them. If a child chooses not to be the character offered to them, we move on to the next child in the circle, and they can say yes or no. Working in this way, I often find that the desire to be on the stage quickly outweighs the desire to refuse to play certain parts. After a few missed goes, children often join in.

But where the issue is more prevalent, we may need to give more weight to this notion that it's just pretend. Sally Veale describes how she began to broach the subject with her year one children.

> *"At the start of the session, before any story acting had begun, I asked the children how they might show they were 'pretending to be an animal when they were on the stage. The children came up with a huge range of suggestions, from how they moved to the noises they could make and even how they might curl up to go to sleep. This was then extended to fantasy characters – witches, dragons and superheroes – all with similar responses."*

Sally would steer clear of asking how the boys might pretend to be girls for fear of prompting a range of stereotypes. However, as soon as she began her story acting session, she would use the word pretend much more explicitly for each character that came up onto the stage. "Can I see you pretending to be a lion? Can I see you pretending to go down the slide? Can I see you pretending to be Anna?" To Sally's surprise, it worked.

Like Sally, I have seen this happen hundreds of times, where children who would actively question whether it was okay to take a role prescribed for another gender suddenly jump up onto the stage to act out the part without any fear that this wasn't right, or that they would be laughed at by their peers.

Through this subtle reminder that what we are doing when we get onto the stage is only pretend, Sally was able to engage all the children in pretending to be any character they liked. Children could still say no to a part, but they no longer did this as a result of thinking that that part was inappropriate for them.

I have seen boys stand up and pretend to be a princess, happily walking through a forest of trees, and girls punch the air joyfully in their pretend fighting of baddies. Helicopter Stories allows boys and girls to explore roles they might never usually get the opportunity to in their play, with children they might never get the opportunity to play with. Girls get to feel what it is like to be a ninja, use a sword, or catch a robber. Boys get the chance to be a sister, or Peppa Pig jumping in puddles, or the fairy godmother making Cinderella's wish come true.

As Sally Veal says, *"The fact that Ray, one of the most confident and popular boys in my current Year 1 class, will willingly stand up and pretend to be the Mummy, whilst Mandy (the girl he is sat next to) is the Daddy, is a testament to the power of storytelling and story acting."*

When we support our children to embrace, 'it's just pretend', they are able to take risks, try out new experiences and see the world in a new light. It's not a difficult concept, but it opens up a world of pretending for them. And with 'it's just pretend', children don't just get to be people or animals. They can pretend to be a ball bouncing down the street, or piece of paper lying on the ground, or a flickering fire. No longer restrained by convention, imaginations can fly, and then who knows what will we happen next.

After all, 'It's Only Pretend.'